Prelude

I decided to head down there and meet the tenant. Now with me showing up at 6 p.m. the rest of the tenants came out of their apartments to see what was the commotion.

First of all, the smell was nasty so we determined it was coming from this one studio apartment. I knocked on the door but no answer. The tenant that lived there was a quiet gentleman who stayed to himself in the apartment and by day was a trader in the stock market.

As I opened the door there was the tenant sitting naked by his computer desk.

Apparently, that smell was not ethnic food cooking, but a dead body.

The body had been decomposing for four to five days and the maggots were all over his body and in his eyes.

Being a real estate person I was never prepared to find or be in this situation.

However, as you will read, this is just one of many unbelievable stories that I have come across in my career.

Enjoy.

Chapter 1

My Dad & Other Early Influences

I grew up in a northern Rhode Island city named Woonsocket to working class parents with no brothers or sisters. My parents were the best any child could have growing up.

My dad, Albo Cesaroni, nicknamed Bo or BoBo, owned an auto body shop called C&F Auto Sales, a used car lot and C&F car wash on the main thoroughfare called Diamond Hill Road in Woonsocket.

Mom worked in a blanket factory called Stamina Mills and then later in an electronic assembly place called Miller's Electric. Mom worked hard in those places and kept the house organized since Dad worked long hours in the business.

From the beginning their focus was for me to be brought up in that brick cape and follow my parents rules. Being an only child I was very lucky which made my parents strict but not that strict. Still the focus was to behave, do good in school and go to college so mom and dad could be proud.

At ten years old myself and some of the neighborhood kids would go through the woods to the public golf course. The other favorite hang out was the newly built shopping center. You have to realize it was the 60's and groups of different stores in one location was a pretty new concept.

Woonsocket Plaza, as it was called could only lead to trouble and it did. Imagine even back then kids would hang out at the local mall and congregate at their favorite stores.

Some of the kids started stealing stuff like Playboy magazines, candy and an assortment of things from Liggetts Drugs. At Woolworth's retail store which had a lunch counter we would bust balloons to eat one-cent banana splits. Soon we were making counterfeit penny stickers to avoid spending $1.50 - $2.00 for the banana splits.

As it turned out, the golf course ended up being my favorite place. I would either run across two streets to the back of the Woonsocket Plaza and end up at the 18th tee area or go through the woods at the second street and end up on the 11th fairway.

At Winnisuket Country Club I started caddying and worked my way up to a Class "A" caddy. I made friends with the other top caddies which turned out to be a blessing. Back in those days if you were not a good caddy the top caddies would throw you in the 18th pond, which had dark muddy water and a giant snapping turtle. Luckily I was never thrown in.

The caddying experience was right up my alley and this is where at an early age I learned about business.

For example, I never wanted to caddy for the doctors and lawyers because they were the cheap tippers. I made sure I would get the double bags of the real estate developers and the gamblers who gave the biggest tips. They were a bunch of characters who own small businesses in the city like Chevy dealerships, flower shops and construction companies.

There were also prominent doctors, lawyers and politicians. There were also some independently wealthy folks who were full-time golf hustlers.

Now remember this was back in the 60's and the golf matches were $100 nassau's which meant $100 for the front, back and the whole 18 holes. By the end of the matches you could lose $500 for the day.

This caddying business not only worked out well, but it led to other jobs such as cleaning the club house each day and eventually working in the pro shop. The golf pro was a crusty old lovable man named Tony Guimelli, who had nicknames for all the kids like "lover boy," "small change" and "peanut."

At the time, Guimelli was one of the best teaching pros in New England.

Dads with gifted young sons and daughters would bring their children to Guimelli to learn the game through a true professional player.

Tony taught the game, but also instructed his students to learn the mental side of the game and play smart golf. The good young players of today have teams with a swing coach, a mental coach and all the computerized technology to measure their statistics.

When you paid for lessons with Tony, you received tutor ledge from all these individuals.

He was also a pretty damn good player, winning the New England PGA Stroke Play tournament in 1942. Now keep in mind this was a time before the PGA tour was even started.

He would reminisce about a group of great players traveling from town to town playing golf for very small money. He grew up in the Buffalo area and caddied for golf legend Walter Hagen otherwise known as the "Haig."

He would tell me of the times with Walter would shoot a 3 or 4-under par 67. After his round, he would start partying in the clubhouse, go out to dinner with friends, party some more and end up on the first tee the next morning in the same clothes he had on the night before. Tony was amazed at some of the golf shots and Walter taught Tony how to make those shots.

I worked at the club doing three jobs and as a 11-year-old I was making $110-$120 a week and banking every dollar. There was also another advantage, the opportunity to play free golf every night. So after shagging balls for the pro, the three or four of us would play nine holes until it got dark.

The old pro was also very accommodating with me and would give me free golf lessons. I felt very fortunate receiving lessons from this man who was willing to share every piece of knowledge about golf and life.

As the golf course became somewhat of a sanctuary with work and golf, the auto body shop was also a great place.

I worked in the car wash for my dad, back then the car wash cost $1.25 - $1.50 and we would wash between 3,000-4,000 cars per weekend. Dad had all the kids in the neighborhood working for him in the winter time where temperatures were pretty cold and working with water made it feel even colder. My dad loved the kids and they loved him with a mutual respect that sometimes the kids parents never showed.

Imagine this all within walking distance, I had the Winnesucket golf course, auto body shop, an Italian restaurant named the New Moon and the Italian social club called the Italian Workman's Club, where my dad was a member for 40 years.

Dad was one of the founding members of the Thundermist Striper Club which was located in the Italian Workingman's Club. They were very serious fishermen going out to Block Island Sound at 2 a.m. in the morning and hitting the schools of stripers. One year Dad won the prize for the largest striper from a boat which weighted 45 pounds. He also caught a 42, 37, 33-pound fish that same night.

On one lot, dad had the auto body shop which fixed damaged cars, a used car lot which fixed and sold affordable cars to mostly everyone in the neighborhood. Eventually, he put in gas pumps so he could offer a deal with a car wash.

At the Italian Workingman's Club I picked up another job, on Saturday nights by checking coats and picking up glasses for large parties. It was another $50 bucks per week and I would walk home at 2 o'clock in the morning with no fear of danger or ever getting robbed. It was just a great time to be young.

My dad was also quite an outdoorsman with striped bass fishing being the primary activity along with hunting and ice fishing in the winter. During hunting season Dad and his friends would go to Vermont and stay at a friends hunting cabin.

Dad always drove the big Chevy Blazer that was white and gold and he used it for all his outdoor activities. I never forgot the scene of Dad and his friends driving home from Vermont one Saturday morning on Diamond Hill with the largest buck I ever saw strapped to the roof of the blazer.

That day Dad gutted and skinned the deer and brought a large amount of meat to the New Moon restaurant for chef Louie Visicone to prepare a venison dinner for everyone at the Italian Workingman's Club.

Every week in the summer my dad would catch the stripers and my grandma, otherwise known as nonna or nonni, would prepare weekly meals for the family. She would also make homemade macaroni and some wonderful Italian soups. If dad wanted to give nonna a rest he would call Louie at the New Moon restaurant which was located on the side of his business and order the best veal and macaroni for supper.

As you can probably imagine, we were never starving. As I mentioned earlier, Dad was a very generous man and would give the extra fish he caught to the Laotian people in Woonsocket, and they adored him for it.

Matter of fact, when Dad died so many Laotian people showed up at his wake that my wife was thought they might be in the wrong funeral parlor. Her concerns were erased when one of them came up to us and said he was there to pay his respects to Bo Fishman.

Dad had quite a few friends in business and politics. He was a very generous man and was a big supporter of the Democratic Party by fixing local politicians vehicles free of charge. (By the way, the politicians never planned on paying anyway.) Favors were prevalent, and as it turned out, the favors led to quite a nice position in state government after my dad sold the auto body shop, car wash and used car lot.

There were also a whole bunch of other characters who hung out at the auto body shop.

Hunters, fishermen and all types of outdoorsman would gather there bring my dad and the kids coffee and donuts. My dad would buy the kids lunches at the local fast food places. I'm really not sure how my dad got the work done with everyone hanging out, but it got done and it was quite a huge social scene.

One of the funniest stories, or maybe not so funny if you're an animal activist, was the time one of my dad's best fishing buddies came back from hunting. As he pulled up, my dad came outside to meet him and asked "Did you get anything?"

The hunter replied, "Yes, an ostrich."

My dad, looking shocked, cried out, "an ostrich!"

As the hunter opened the trunk of his 1963 Chevrolet Impala, there laid a dead ostrich. My dad, still in amazement told him firmly to get that fucking thing out of here. Apparently the ostrich escaped from Bensons Wild Animal farm in Uxbridge, Massachusetts.

As Dad was told, the ostrich attacked the hunter and had to be shot. This was the same person who put marijuana in my dad's pipe while they were fishing out in the boat.

The summer time was great. We would play golf every night and hang around the golf club. I would get my work done and we would have putting contests on the practice green at the top of the hill.

It was also a fantastic time for cookouts at my mom and dad's place since they had a large half acre back yard. All the relatives were there with everyone bringing food to help my mom. Again, there was never a shortage of food and drink and talk of politics and the sharing of funny stories from everyone.

One of my dad's best friends and neighbors Don Picchoni would host political parties at his large house/yard where all the folks would gather for food, drink, and chat with state and local politicians.

There was a big concrete pool with a ton of people cooling off from the hot summer sun. It was a great time. Don, who made concrete pipes for the City of Woonsocket, was a very generous man and during the time Dad sold his business as he allowed my Dad to set up an auto body shop in one of the garages on his property for free.

By now I'm sure you realize this was a different era than today and people were generous and down to earth, always willing to care about one another.

When I started driving at 15-years-old, my dad would have me pick up auto parts for the auto body shop. Walking was now a thing of the past.

We soon started to explore new areas and learned the road system and where it would take us. I bought my first car, in cash, from my Dad which was a 1969 Camaro with Brown exterior and white vinyl roof. The interior had white leather seats and a black/brown dashboard.

It was a cool car.

Every weekend we would travel to the different golf courses and play 18-holes. Just a great time to be young.

One of the favorite places was the local race track, Lincoln Downs (now Twin River), and soon I was going there to place bets for Tony Guimelli.

Back then it was a horse racing track for thoroughbreds and it eventually became a dog track before giving way to a slot parlor and casino. It was a blast placing bets with little money we had and sometimes winning and losing.

One of the local kids from the neighborhood worked at the track and owned a race horse named Bambulane and the horse won its only race at 15-1 odds and we all bet it. One kid hit the daily double and made $1,500. Most of us bet it to win, place and show and made some good spending money.

Within a couple of years of obtaining my driver's license, the drinking age changed to 18-years-old and we were able to hang at the local bars and clubs.

I'll never forget a local establishment named Kozy Bar on Social Street in Woonsocket. It was just a dive, but had a shuffle board table the length of the bar and a bowling pin game where you threw a metal disc to try to knock down as many pins as you could.

The best thing about the bar was the draft beer. It was ten cents for a 12-ounce draft beer. We would drink in there for hours for a total of $1.50 each.

At 18, I co-captained the Woonsocket High School golf team with another senior named Tommy Wecal. We grew up together in the same neighborhood and became great friends.

Tommy was just an outstanding athlete, also co-captaining high school hockey team.

We played our home matches at Winnesuket Country Club and were a very good team, shooting an average score of 76-77 for 18 holes.

In our freshmen year four of our players won the Northwestern Division and made it to the State Finals. We lost the medal play tournament and only won the division the next two years, but never made it any further.

Anyway, so much for the early success. Still it was one of the best times of my life.

That September, I was off to college at Wentworth Institute of Technology.

The college experience was so much different than living at home where all my meals were served to me and all my clothes were cleaned each day.

My first year I lived in the new dormitory the college built for all incoming freshman.

One of the new experiences was actually living with a roommate. I got very lucky since my new roommate did not like the dormitory, leaving me along by by myself in a nice new dormitory room.

It was great for studying and made quite a lot of new friends. One in particular was Bruce Beaumont from Narragansett, Rhode Island and we are still the best of friends today.

I started out in a civil engineering program but eventually changed to industrial / mechanical engineering.

My thought process was that construction jobs were unstable and manufacturing in America was here to stay.

Boy, was I incorrect on that one.

One of my best experiences I had in college was meeting a cute blond haired girl named Beverly Saltonstall that lived in Mapleville, Rhode Island, the most northern part of the state.

During the summer of second year and my dad, through his political connections, got me a state government job. Expecting an engineering job in road construction like I had my first summer my dad told me that all the engineering jobs were taken.

As he said "I got some good news and some bad news. The good news is you have a job. The bad news is its at the The Zambarano Mental Health hospital for long term care."

Here we go again, but as it turned out I met this girl who was becoming a nursing major at the University of Rhode Island. She eventually became my wife of 38-years and we blessed our moms and dads with a beautiful baby girl, who is now 28 and armed with degrees, a great job and fiercely independent.

Anyway, I made it through four years of college and received my Bachelors degree. I was ready to start my career.

It was 1976 and jobs were very scarce.

Even though the Vietnam War was over, un-employment was very high and most companies were still trying to find their niche in the business world.

Engineering opportunities were few and far between, and with my dad's connections, I started on the second shift at a plastic injection molding company named the Tupperware Company.

I was a mechanic and troubleshooter on the injection molding machines and adapted very quickly to the working world. It was an interesting environment where savvy working women ran the machines and if they didn't like you they would let you know it.

I found myself being well liked by helping them out running the machines. Most of them were twice my age, some were much older and even knew my mother.

I was promoted after three years to the quality control department and worked in the color matching lab and a skunk works project making dishwasher safe material. The job was actually very interesting and I learned a lot.

My dad's connection in the company was the Vice President of Engineering Richard Anterni who was a toolmaker by trade. He designed and tooled all of the injection molds.

My dad knew him from the old neighborhood where he and his brother ran a machine shop. Matter of fact, as I progressed in my electronics career I helped Richard Anterni's son Peter find his first job at ACT Manufacturing where I was a Material Manager.

I worked for the Vice President of Quality Control, Bob Gosselin, who started at the bottom of the company as an assembler and worked his way up to learn the whole business. He was just a great mentor in this company and it did not hurt he was also great friends with Richard Anterni. They would travel the world together for the company which had plants every where in the world.

He was divorced, but was dating his assistant, a pretty short hair blonde who eventually became his wife.

Everyone knew to stay on her good side or she could make life a living hell. I stayed at this company approximately three years and moved on to a worldwide company called Motorola.

I was a manufacturing engineer in the cable/wire harness area and worked for a guy named Art Napoleone. Art was a smart individual and had plans to move up the corporate ladder fairly quickly. Unfortunately, he had an accident at his house falling off the back deck and hurting his back.

He was out of work for quite awhile and was replaced as our Engineering Manager with a person named Fred Friedenfeld.

Fred was one of the best managers you could have and you always knew where you stood with Fred. Myself and two other engineers named Mike Conley and Hans Grabau became well-liked by Fred and the feeling was mutual. Fred could always count on us doing the right thing for the business.

Fred retired to South Carolina with his wife and still calls each one of us yearly. The three of us still keep in touch today, and as I said earlier, these were great relationships we all kept during our working careers.

Today, friendships such as we had rarely last 25-30 years.

At Motorola we were on the cutting edge of every high technology business you could imagine. Every high technology business around today in 2018 started as a skunk works project at various Motorola locations all around the United States.

A skunk works project was an offline business process for a new technology development that had its own separate group of engineers and managers monitoring it.

Basically, it was a testing of new product development without the pressure of messing up or senior management intervention.

It was great fun and we all made a ton of lifelong friends. Today, I still play golf and go to dinner with almost all of them.

Motorola was so progressive back then, they even asked workers during their review cycle if you wanted to go into management or the technical route. I chose the managerial route and was placed in a supply chain management group to learn a new business. Motorola paid for me to go back to school. As a result, I received an MBA that was paid for entirely by Motorola.

The career change was a great move and after leaving Motorola, the supply chain field became my full time profession for the next 25 years.

Chapter 2

Introduction to Real Estate

As an engineer at Motorola, my work was really interesting, but there was something missing. Maybe it was the entrepreneurial blood from my dad wanting to get out and to do something else part time. The supply chain field as a material manager was very rewarding. This contract manufacturer of printed circuit boards and cable / harnesses grew very quickly and the managerial staff enjoyed some nice benefits.

My dad's cousin Bruno Santini was an insurance salesman for New York Life Insurance Company, but was also a part time real estate agent.

Bruno was a tall, opposing man who was devoted to his family, with three children, a beautiful wife and many friends and connections to the old country.

Back then insurance salesmen figured if people buy insurance eventually they will buy a house. So a lot of them had both insurance and real estate licenses.

Bruno worked for a small mom and pop real estate agency called Cumberland Hill Realty in Cumberland, Rhode Island, the next town over.

The owners, Roland and Marlene Gagnon, were friends of Bruno, and also were in the insurance business with John Hancock Life Insurance.

The Gagnon's were lovely people. Roland was of French – Canadian descent and Marlene was of Italian heritage. Actually, my dad knew her side of the family very well from the old neighborhood.

Bruno introduced me to them, and a lifelong friendship was born.

To work for them I had to go to school at Rhode Island Junior College (now CCRI) and get my real estate license, which I did and started my new part time career in real estate sales. Due to the time constraints of having a full time job, I focused my real estate career on nights, weekends and holidays.

As Roland and Marlene expanded their real estate portfolio I worked in the sales office making cold calls and setting up meetings with folks who might be interested in selling or listing their houses.

By this time, Roland and Marlene Gagnon had acquired 17 multi-family homes and 105 apartment units. The real estate business was very good to them in the 1970's and supported their only daughter Michelle in private school and four years of college.

The part time career was turning out to be a very rewarding experience

My real estate sales increased to selling and/or listing five to ten houses per year.

My wife and I had made a deal that any money from real estate would go to buying things for the house and life in general. So we bought home furnishings, new cars and took vacations to warm destinations in the winter.

Life was pretty darn good.

Besides the sales end, I was also learning property management from Roland by working at the office. I paid attention to every detail.

The Gagnon's were amazing for just a husband/wife team and a general maintenance person. They successfully ran 17 properties in the late 70's and early 80's.

The 105 apartment rentals had to be maintained every day because of broken pipes, water/sewer back ups, electrical problems and leaking roofs. By the way, the vacancies had to be filled with new tenants so there would be a steady stream of income to pay the mortgages and other monthly bills.

So as I learned at Motorola the same applied to real estate, that there was a business process that needed to be followed.

It was not so much as to which person to call, but the key was to have an experienced general maintenance person to assess the situation so the owners would not have to spend a lot of money trying to determine the real cause of the problem.

The Gagnon's also maintained vendor lists, or people they could call at a moments notice to fix any emergencies associated with building maintenance.

They also used their connections to keep a waiting list of people looking for apartments.

Matter of fact, the Gagnon's purchased mostly all of their properties through local French-Canadian contacts in the city of Woonsocket of people reportedly wanting to sell.

Marlene was very proficient in keeping detailed records and maintaining the books to track the income and expenses of the real estate business.

Keep in mind, cell phones were only starting to make their way into the business arena so all the calls came in while I was in the office on weekends, nights and holidays.

Today, smart phones have really changed the real estate business and saved time and energy of property managers.

The biggest improvement has been in tenant communications because of the ability to send mass text messages.

Chapter 3

The Fixer Upper

As the Gagnon's started to get older they also decided to downsize their portfolio because of a divorce situation and eliminate the real estate sales business.

My family was brought up in Greenville, Rhode Island, away from the real estate company so I started looking at different real estate companies to hang my license. What I found was most real estate firms did not want to hire part time agents that way the full timers could make a decent living.

In my travels around northern Rhode Island, I located a real estate firm, Berthod Real Estate, in the same building as my attorney. It was there that I met a wonderful gentleman, Lou Berthod. He was kind, funny and took me under his wing allowing me to hang my license at his office.

Lou was a very savvy experienced real estate person who was very detailed oriented in putting together a real estate deal. His prime activity was selling houses but he also dealt in commercial buildings, raw land conversion and elderly / HUD housing developments.

My new found real estate boss became one of my best friends and introduced me to Kirkbrae Country Club a private golf club located in Lincoln, Rhode Island where we played primarily on weekends. The club is where I am still a member today after 18 years and have made some wonderful friends.

Lou and his family owned a lake house on Spring Lake in Burrillville, Rhode Island and would throw great parties. We would cruise around on his pontoon boat with Lou wearing the skippers hat while listening to Dean Martin CD's and having a few drinks.

At this point in time, my father had passed away and my mother had moved into an elderly complex where her sister lived. She was still driving so she could babysit my daughter, who was 6-years-old and getting ready to start school.

My mother in law was a tough Russian woman who also babysat my daughter, so we were in a great situation. My daughter was being taken care of by her two grandmothers, my wife was a Nursing Manager and I worked in the supply chain field for ACT Manufacturing.

Lou was starting to convince me to invest in real estate for my future and build equity in real estate. He always said the real estate rental income would be forever and would supplement my retirement income along with social security.

It made perfect sense since most corporations now were downsizing and eliminating jobs. Pension benefits were disappearing with most of the positions going overseas.

One weekend while working in Lou's office, he gave me a real estate listing in Glocester Rhode Island just up the road from where I lived.

It was a rundown 16 unit building with all one bedroom apartments. The owners were funeral directors and thought they could get rich very quickly by buying real estate.

Unfortunately, they were not real estate savvy and just wanted to unload the property.

They wanted $550,000 and Lou made an offer of $480,000 on my behalf.

They accepted the offer and my real estate investment journey began.

I had a small inheritance and with my own funds I made a 20 percent down payment and financed the rest through a bank. We closed at the end of May and I had my attorney form a LLC company.

LLC's are mostly formed for real estate partnerships to protect people's personal assets. One of the difficult parts with a real estate investment of this kind is the amount of time you have to be devote to protect your investment.

With that in mind, Lou had recommended that his son Tony manage the building for me and be the property manager.

Tony worked as a property manager for a Boston-based Housing and Urban Development (HUD) company named The Community Builders and would manage my building. He was in need of a part time job because he just had been through a nasty divorce and had three children.

The kids were just starting their teenage years and Tony felt they needed a father figure in their lives. Tony also enlisted a maintenance supervisor named Paul Morin at one of the properties he managed to be the general maintenance person for my building. Paul is still with me today and turned out to be one of the best general maintenance people you can have in the business. Talk about a small world Paul learned the business working for my dad's cousin who built houses in Bellingham, Massachusetts in the 60's and 70's.\

The building had a brick and vinyl exterior, but the roof was in desperate need of repair.

So the first thing we did was hire a roofing contractor through three bids and chose the best price that met the specifications. Within a week the building had a new roof and Paul and Tony were ready to tackle the interior.

Out of the 16 units, nine were rented, so the first thing Tony did was to get everyone to sign a one-year lease with a rent increase of $25.00 per month.

If you did not sign the lease and wanted a month-to-month tenancy it was an increase of $50-$75.00 per month depending on where your unit was located in the building.

First-floor units were more expensive than the second-floor units due to the layout of the building and the first-floor units had more square footage. Surprisingly all nine tenants signed the one year lease and we had steady cash flow to pay the bills.

We decided to use a templet for the interiors and the biggest bang for our buck was to focus on apartment turnovers on three interior elements: paint, carpets and appliances.

So we started with the first unit which was kind of small, but we upgraded it and found out by advertising, we could raise the rent from $500 to $650-$675 per month, and so the base price for our second-floor units were set lower.

The money began to flow in and we soon realized we had a full fledged real estate business in the works. Part of the reason for the increased cash flow was the fact we had private water and sewer which was much cheaper than public services. The heat was electric and all paid by tenants so that also helped.

Tony was happy getting 10 percent of the monthly gross rents as his fee but he also had full property management responsibilities.

Paul was happy to get paid $25 per hour, per job and have the extra income along with his regular maintenance job.

Overall, we all learned a lot about each other including each persons strengths and weaknesses. For example, Paul knew general maintenance and was excellent at fixing problems to save material and labor costs.

Tony had a great deal of property management experience, but he also had the right attitude to deal with tenants.

Both of these attributes taught me how this real estate business should be run, and also helped me to learn the financial end of the business.

Landlords have free rein to set the market conditions on apartment rentals and no governing body in the world has any authority to enforce it. But you know what, with a little paint and some updates we were doing something about it and that made us feel pretty damn good that we offered affordable apartment rentals.

One element we haven't talked about is the tenants, who basically are our customers and pay our mortgage. We quickly learned the tenant profile for our building which was divorced, empty nesters or just couples looking for affordable living.

The tenants in this building were very interesting.

For example, one Asian woman and her daughter had more "stuff" in this small one bedroom apartment than anyone I have ever seen.

Items included a Buddhist temple in her living room, along with a fish tank and a 70-inch flat screen television.

During one fire inspection the fire marshal spoke to me outside and said, "Do you believe that apartment?"

As it turns out, the mother moved to this country from Asia provide a better life for her daughter.

Apparently, the mother would store goods in her apartment and send to her struggling parents in Asia.

Her daughter ended up getting into college.

Another interesting tenant was a single young man with a medical marijuana card.

He told me he was allowed to keep a two-foot plant in his apartment making the hallway smell pretty good with that aroma.

I actually was thinking about speaking to him since I had four acres on the property and maybe a distribution business could be in our future.

Another tenant was a stripper at the local adult entertainment place in Rhode Island. She would also pay her rent in cash with very small bills.

She started out never being late on a rent payment, but issues with her boyfriend and the police having to intervene violated her lease agreement. She then escalated the issue by making her personal issues the landlords problem.

In this particular case, the woman did not pay her rent by the 15th of the month and so we sent her what is known in the business as a five day demand letter to evict by the 21st.

Once the tenant receives the letter I, or in this case, Tony would go and have a conversation with the apartment tenant.

If the rent was not received by the 21st my attorney would receive the demand letter and eviction proceedings would start with a court date.

The key for the landlord to save some money is to get the tenant to move out before the court date. If this does not happen than you have to hire the sheriff and the movers and by time your done and have your apartment back in your possession your $2,000 down.

Luckily, she moved out before the court date and we saved some money.

One of the most interesting things as a landlord that I had to deal was a tenant who died in the apartment.

I definitely have more gruesome stories later in the book. This tenant had a massive heart attack in the apartment and luckily his brother found his body a day later before it had any chance of decomposing.

Still, it was a traumatic experience with someone dying in your property.

The Medical examiner and State Police had to investigate, and there are cleaning companies which only worked for the State of Rhode Island to clean up these messes.

Some of the tenants have unusual requests when moving in.

One such request came from a family that actually worked on a horse farm in Glocester and were of Bolivian heritage. Since they worked on a horse farm all day where dirt, horse droppings and hay were a fact of life, they requested all the carpets be removed and replaced with linoleum upon moving in.

As it turned out, the carpets were pretty worn so my maintenance guy had the whole apartment done in linoleum and we found out it was about 30-40 percent cheaper than carpets.

They turned out to be wonderful tenants and paid on the first of each month.

The other challenge with tenants especially with single folks and empty nesters is everyone had a pet.

Back when I first started in the business, I could rent to anyone that had a dog, but as time went on insurance companies started warning landlords about renting to tenants with dogs over 50 pounds, and especially pit bulls.

Based on the tenant profile of this specific building most of my potential tenants had pets, and older women loved their cats. So with every lease agreement we had the tenant sign a Pet Addendum with a one time charge of $200 per pet that was non-refundable. This allowed me to expand my potential tenant market and everyone was happy.

I still rented to tenants with dogs, but was very cautious.

Matter of fact, when Tony showed the apartment and it became evident that they had a dog, Tony would ask them to bring the dog to the showing and he would make a call based on the pet's behavior.

Another lesson Tony and myself learned was regarding late paying tenants.

First of all we heard every excuse in the book, but between the both of us we learned a technique that I still use today with 30 units and no debt collection issues. Its called communication between you and your tenants.

The more communication you and the tenant have the better chance you will get paid.

Coming from working class families we understood folks can easily get into situations when they cannot pay on the first of the month. So if the tenant cannot pay the full rent on the first, we always wrote the rent receipt for some of it and documented the balance due by the fifteenth of the month.

At this point in time, a personal conversation with the tenant regarding the five day demand letter and the amount of the balance would take place prior to the fifteenth of the month.

I would say 99 percent of the time we had the rent before the fifteenth due to a little scare tactic we used by warning the tenant, "You really do not want an eviction on your record to ruin your credit."

Let's face it, that once percent were never going to pay so you either start the eviction process or they moved out.

Tenant turnover is really not a bad thing for a landlord. If the apartment is still in good shape you have the maintenance person clean it up and shampoo the rugs and you rent it for more money and give yourself a raise.

Within two years the building was always fully rented bringing in maximum cash flow and the equity was increasing in a real estate market that was also seeing some phenomenal growth.

As my old mentors the Gagnons used to say, "the real estate cycle was a seven year cycle and landlords made money just from economic activity."

After 20 years in this business, the same holds true and I have always believed in that rule.

Chapter 4

The Impact of the Station Night Club Fire

As I previously mentioned, my original mentors the Gagnons were divorced and downsizing their portfolio in 2001.

Marlene called me one day and I drove to her house and we started talking about me purchasing her two six-unit buildings in Woonsocket, where bars and tenement houses were around every corner.

I had some money, but I also had a substantial 401K built up at Motorola where I still worked full time. Now, understand that every accountant and financial planner tells you not to pull money from these accounts, but I did anyway.

In my early 40s, my thought process was if I was going to be committed to the real estate business for the long hall I would get that money back during my lifetime.

The bad news is that I was penalized, but the good news was I had enough money from the 401K for the down payment and to pay the penalty.

We closed fairly quickly.

By January of 2001 my portfolio was up to 28 apartment rentals, which for a small investor had some pretty good income.

I learned that investing in two, three and four unit buildings is not a bad real estate investment, but the cash flow is very limited if you have any vacancies. The larger units help buffer you from any vacancies, but also allows you to pay the bills much easier.

Soon after we closed on the 12 units, tragedy struck Rhode Island in the form of Station Night Club Fire.

The Station Night Club was a popular club in West Warwick, Rhode Island that featured live music from some of the most popular bands in the state and across New England on a weekly basis.

I had never been to the Station Night Club, but had heard a lot about it.

On the night of February 20, 2003, with the band Great White headlining, the band's tour manager set off pyrotechnics inside the building which ignited plastic foam used as sound insulation in the walls and ceilings surrounding the stage. The fire took less than six minutes to spread, killing 100 people and injuring 230, while 132 escaped the building uninjured.

At the time, it was the fourth deadliest nightclub fire in U.S. History, and the second deadliest in New England.

It took the State of Rhode Island an entire year to pass new fire code regulations and in that time all I, as a landlord, could do was wait.

Once the codes were finally passed, we had to move right away or else contractors would raise prices very quickly to take advantage of the new regulations.

Luckily, landlords that had residential real estate such as apartment units were spared and no sprinklers were necessary, but the buildings had to have hardwired smoke alarms with control fire box units in the basements.

All landlords were also required to have quarterly inspections in all units.

I knew the new fire code regulations would cost all landlords across the state more money, but I was committed to do anything I needed to do to make my buildings safe.

Tony had recommended a small company out of Warwick, named Electronic Alarms, which I still use to this day. They have since been acquired by a larger firm out of Boston, but in my mind they still give me the same incredible service and we are on a first name basis.

They installed a state of the art system for 2003 and all the tenants in the building were very happy.

The next upgrade that had to be done was to make the buildings lead safe. This was a key factor for marketing the units to families with children.

So being pro-active, Tony and myself went to classes to become Certified Lead Inspectors and earned our certificates. Our maintenance person, Paul, who had a contractor's license worked on a price to install Harvey Replacement windows.

The issue was we needed 136 of them. So with Paul getting us the contractor discounts and doing the installations we ended up with some pretty good pricing.

This would normally have been a $70,000 job, but we turned it into a $35,000 job. Besides that, Tony and myself were the lead inspectors for each apartment which saved us a total of $2,400 or $200 per apartment.

The first thing we had to do was encapsulate each window which was being installed.

So we rented the biggest dumpster we could find from the local wrecking company and placed it in the driveway between the two houses.

We started on the third floor and as Paul and his team took out the old windows, they threw it out the opening and into the dumpster below.

Once this was done the window frame was cleaned and Tony and myself applied the dust wipes and secured them in a container for transport to the lab.

This process took approximately two weeks, but we had all new vinyl replacement windows rather than the old aluminum ones. It was great in the winter to hold in the heat.

The families in both buildings loved it.

As we made the improvements we also developed the tenant profile for this property. There were five two-bedrooms and one one-bedroom per building.

The current tenant base was older French –Canadian mill workers, some of whom had their children living with them. We made some small rent adjustments and had a couple of vacancies among the larger two bedroom units.

We used the Providence Journal for unfurnished apartments, which turned out to be a more reliable source for quality phone calls. The internet was free, but most of the folks were pretty unsure of where they really wanted to live in Rhode Island. The ads were very straight forward with the highway access, address, price and what it includes. One ad usually generated ten phone calls.

Half of the calls would come in while the ad was running and the other half came after it ran out.

One of the advantages with the Journal was that you not only get seven days in the paper, but also nine days on the internet for $141.60 per ad.

We started to change the tenant base and had some real interesting characters.

One particular one was Florence who had a deep French Canadian accent.

I think she came with the purchase of the buildings and was a Section 8 tenant for 20 years. She has now been there 37 years and pays $300 per month for a nice one bedroom. At 89-years-old she sweeps the parking lot and keeps her independence.

Her children want her to move, but everyone in the building watches out for Florence's welfare. She keeps telling me she will die there.

Chapter 5
The Tenants From Hell

For all the great tenants that I have had over my career, there are always a few that I wish I never dealt with.

One French Canadian couple named Bob and Claudette were very cordial and nice when I bought the building. They kept telling me their rent was too high at $700 per month with heat and hot water.

Now you have to understand, this was a first-floor front apartment with the large double parlor with two bedrooms, kitchen and bath. These units rent today at $850-$900 a month due to their size and location in the building.

Unfortunately, I had to raised everyone's rent including Bob and Claudette's to $750 per month with heat and hot water. Now they were always telling me their name was on a waiting list for elderly housing in Woonsocket.

This couple lived a life of modest means, but they were very intelligent and sly.

Their attire consisted of sweat shirts, jeans and sneakers every day, but one particular incident was really confusing.

Apparently, as they were going out one night Claudette fell on the front walk and broke her ankle. She was in an ankle cast for six weeks and soon after the accident I received a certified letter from an attorney suing my LLC for not maintaining the front walkway.

I had Paul assess the situation to find out the condition of the walkway. He soon came back stating nothing was wrong, no broken cement, but as most walkways have expansion joints in the concrete to allow for expansion during hot and cold temperatures.

The interesting part of this case was Claudette, who I never saw in anything but sneakers, broke her ankle that night wearing high heels and the heel of the shoe lodged into the expansion joint, she twisted her ankle and the rest is history.

My insurance settled the case for $35,000 and I took a hit on my premium.

Bob and Claudette eventually got senior housing and I updated the apartment with paint/carpet and re-rented it for $800 per month with heat and hot water included to a nice Mexican family.

My years in the business were very fortunate since I never took anyone to court, but owning this property that was about to change very quickly. You have to understand Woonsocket is a melting pot of all different ethnic groups which provides great rental opportunities for landlords but the different cultures produce many different personalities.

Growing up in the same neighborhood my attitude was that all people were good. As a kid this close knit Italian community did change over time, but only with different ethnic groups, the people remained the same.

We rented to a fine well spoken Nigerian gentlemen whose background checks came back excellent.

The first couple of months were fine, but then there were problems collecting the rent.

As the months went on, there were more excuses with his bank screwing up and he expected money from his country that never came to him. He would pay the rent, but it was just harder to collect as the months went on.

He knew the system pretty well and would have the full rent by the fifteenth of the month so I could never drag him into court. Eventually there was no communication with this gentleman and we would knock on his door with no answer.

Tony found out through some friends at Bureau of Crime Investigation (BCI) there was an arrest warrant out for his arrest for drug trafficking so we took him to court. He never showed up and the judge gave us possession of the apartment.

That morning we had Paul change the locks and hired a company to take all of the man's belongings out of the apartment and bring it to the dump. This is not the normal process, if the tenant is in the apartment legally you hire the sheriff and a moving company to store the goods until they are sold six months later.

We figured that due to the drug charge he was never coming back so we saved some money to just dispose of his stuff.

Tony and I always had a quick rule in renting to folks that wanted to give you the security deposit and rent money very quickly. It was definitely a red flag for potential trouble.

We had a very thorough application process and we asked straight forward questions. If anyone did not want to fill in all the information we knew it could be a potential problem. Over the years we developed a technique that had the potential tenant fill out the application and then we would run criminal, credit and sex offender background checks.

It would take two days and we would get back to the potential tenant and let them know if they are approved or disapproved.

During one of the severe winters we had a vacancy in one of the buildings on the second floor. We put an ad in the paper and received five or six calls, which were pretty good considering the weather.

We ended up choosing a woman who worked part time and collected about $900 per month on Social Security Disability Insurance (SSDI). She was very kind and fun loving with a small dog and just seemed like she enjoyed life. Not a career girl, but she did the best she could do.

After a few months everything changed and she became the tenant from hell.

We had another vacancy across the hall from her and filled it with a military veteran that was injured during the Gulf War and worked at the veteran's organization Operation Stand Down.

What we did not know about the girl was that she was bi-polar and in the past had been committed to Butler Hospital, the state's mental hospital.

She also played the system very well by having the full rent by the fifteenth of the month. Apparently, she created many disturbances at the apartment with her undesirable friends and the Woonsocket Police had to calm everyone down. We also suspected drugs were involved.

Now the story really gets interesting.

During one of her bi-polar episodes she started stalking the military veteran from across the hall. In one instance, she actually threw paint all over this tenants door and on the hallway floor.

At this point, the police and mental heath advisor committed her to Butler again for a two week period. It was no surprise that when she came out her rent was not paid by the middle of the month. My attorney acted quickly and we served her with a court date. She did not show up so the judge gave us possession of the apartment.

We took this all the way and hired the sheriff and Woonsocket Police to escort her from the apartment and the movers placed all her belongings in storage.

She continued to call my attorney to retrieve some of her belongings because there was a laptop computer she wanted. My attorney politely requested a certified check of $2,000 paid to me to get her stuff released.

We never saw any money. I re-rented the apartment to two Mexican gentlemen who worked in construction with my other second floor tenant.

We ended up getting $50.00 more per month and finally got rid of the wacky woman.

Now remember the military gentleman from across the hall who was being stalked by the crazy woman? Well, he also started to fall behind in his rent payments.

I could not make this stuff up.

As previously mentioned he worked for Operation Stand Down and one of his roles was to be a part time drug informant for the police. It's all coming together and the reason for the crazy woman stalking him was that he sold drugs to her and her friends. Once the her supply of drugs was shut off, she went crazy.

Anyway, we started to chase him for the rent and for a couple of months the veteran's organization would actually pay his rent in full. He started to become unruly with loud screaming fits and it was the first time in my life I realized I could be in a dangerous situation and might be attacked.

Eventually, I had enough and the following month I only received a partial rent payment. I quickly had my attorney serve him and we had about six months of five- day demand letters for the judge to witness.

Apparently, he showed up at court and was very apprehensive about going in front of the judge. The reason was he had a prior domestic assault charge many years ago.

The judge reviewed the documentation and gave us possession of the apartment. While waiting for the eviction notice to be processed, which is a five day waiting period, something strange happened.

This tenant created a disturbance with a woman in his apartment and the police arrived and found a loaded musket rifle in the bedroom. The police quickly arrested him and sent him to the ACI which is the state prison.

I'm not sure how this individual made bail, but once released he called me to open up his apartment because my maintenance man locked the door during his prison stay.

Legally, I could not change the locks since the eviction notice was still being processed. So we talked about opening his apartment and I called for a police escort to let him in. He started mumbling something and the police told him to shut up as the apartment was open.

After a couple of days, the sheriff, Woonsocket Police and the movers knocked on his door and escorted him from the apartment and the police gave him a ride to wherever he was going. After that the movers were done they came up to me and gave me some more strange news.

They could not move his mattress because it had bed bugs!

So now we had to hire a pest control company to fumigate the whole six unit building.

Bed bugs tend to move from apartment to apartment so every unit had to be done. The other tenants were a little annoyed since they had to be out of their apartment for six hours. After they were done my maintenance person and carpet guy bought huge plastic bags to enclose the mattress and brought it to the dump. It turned out to be a successful extermination and the bed bugs were gone.

We started the turnover process by painting and installing all new carpeting then rented the apartment to a fine elderly gentleman.

Since the military veteran never paid the electric bill, we ended up receiving $100 more for the unit and the new tenant paid for electric.

The gentleman was working for the Salvation Army in Providence and was part of a program where the Department of Children Youth and Families (DCYF) found apartments for workers.

DCYF paid his security and first two months rent so we were approved by the State of Rhode Island for $2,400 which was the security, first months rent and one extra month rent.

We figured the $2,400 upfront paid for the bed bugs and with the increased rent, we received approximately $2,100 more per year.

It was quite a relief after dealing with the tenant who could have been quite dangerous.

We turned a very bad situation into a pretty good real estate deal. One of the most valuable real estate lessons I learned from Roland and Marlene Gagnon and from Lou Bethod was if you can overcome the obstacles and resolve tenant concerns it's a pretty good business.

Chapter 6

Dead Bodies, Snakes & Northern RI's Prized Property

The Gagnons were getting up there in age by this time. Marlene contacted me one Saturday and I went to her house in Cumberland. We were always close because of our family history so we sat down and she wanted me to buy her 18 unit brick schoolhouse in Lincoln, Rhode Island.

She was approached by every prominent real estate developer and agency in northern Rhode Island to sell. She always felt I would keep it as apartment rentals which I did. The purchased price back in 2007 was $1.0 million dollars.

I thought not bad for a caddy from Winnesuket Country Club with 46 apartment units and a full time job. She wanted to structure the deal where she would be my silent partner and offered me a 4% loan for half of the purchase price.

This also protected her from state and federal taxes on $500,000 which could be in excess of $150,000 in taxable liability. It also gave her a monthly income the rest of her life to run her housing needs and let her money grow.

So now my real estate mind went to work and my first thoughts was to refinance my existing units.

Keep in mind that over the years I have pulled money out for building improvements and my original investments in my Glocester and Woonsocket properties.

The schoolhouse was built in 1912 and was originally elementary school in Manville Rhode Island. It was a spectacular property.

It actually had a bell tower, with a huge bell that was made by Holbrook Manufacturing in 1879. Holbrook, was the company that made bells for Paul Revere during his midnight ride.

Recently, my wife and I did some research and found that the bell was worth about $25,000. However to sell it, it was going to be a huge undertaking.

We would have to take the roof off the cupola and hire a crane company to remove the bell assembly. This assembly was comprised of huge wooden beams and a spin wheel which moved the bell back and forth.

Once the crane lifted the bell assembly out of the bell tower a flat bed truck would have to be there to drive it to wherever the investor was located.

I estimate that it would have cost me about $5,000 to remove the bell.

The schoolhouse was converted to an apartment building in 1978 by a Woonsocket builder and purchased by the Gagnons in 1982 while I was working for them. The building is also on the Federal Historical Register along with that section of Manville, Rhode Island.

The 16-unit building in Glocester that I originally purchased for $480,000 was now appraising out at $960,000. We also increased the gross rental income by 2.5 times so the cash flow was supporting both properties we owned.

The refinance of the 16-unit building was fairly simple and we pulled out $180,000 in tax free cash and used that money as the down payment for the schoolhouse.

Marlene provided secondary financing for the balance and by March of 2007 we owned the Schoolhouse Apartments LLC. We signed a promissory note for the portion she financed and put her daughter Michelle as the benefiduary in case Marlene died.

At this point Tony, my property manager, had a new girlfriend and needed to devote more time to his full time career. So we decided to have him train my wife Beverly. The process took six months and Beverly turned out to be a great addition for the business.

The building had a 70's décor, so the first thing we did was to eliminate the orange shag carpeting in the common areas. We replaced it with a nice auburn carpet which matched the waistcoating and walls. The apartments were in very good shape and all tenants were hit with a small rental increase.

We had a couple of turnovers, but as we did with our other properties we could increase the rental income and improve cash flow.

One nice cost savings with the Schoolhouse was that Marlene had already fire coded the building, saving us $40,000. I had the lead inspections done for rental marketability.

The lead paint laws grandfathered this building since the conversion to apartments was done in 1978 when the lead paint laws went into effect. As turnovers occurred we stuck to our original model with paint, flooring and appliances. The rental income started to increase significantly and the value of the building also increased.

One thing about apartment rentals is once you increase rents the value of the building increases exponentially. For example, if your building generates $100,000 in rental income the value of that building is $1 million.

Now think about it, every dollar in increased rents you not only get it in the value of the building, but you also make greater income. And that's not all, the best kept secret in real estate is once equity is built you can refinance that building and all the cash is tax free.

How many businesses will allow you that flexibility? Not many.

The first winter we owned the Schoolhouse was a terrible one. We probably had 50 inches of snow and vehicles from nearby rental units were having their tenants park in my parking lot which is obviously private property. We contracted with a towing company and had both vehicles towed to the company lot.

A couple days later this person with a shovel came to retrieve his vehicle and was told they were towed to the company lot. Even with private property signs posted on the front entrance some folks just don't get it.

The rental market around 2006-2007 started to contract and rents were starting to flatten out or even decrease in specific areas. We started to look at all expenses and see where we could save some money.

For instance, instead of having the trash picked up weekly we had it done bi-weekly for three dumpsters. Instead of paying $4,800 per year for each dumpster the bi-weekly schedule decreased each dumpster to $2,400 each per year.

Total savings: $7,200 per year.

The next thing we did was hire my electrician to update all the timers in each of building's common areas. He also synchronized all the timers to save on the electric bills for the common areas.

Our heating contractor cleaned our boilers to make sure they were running efficiently so heating cost would not be out of sight.

Another cost saving trick we realized was to read the water meter once a month for Narragansett Bay Commission (NBC). NBC is the agency which cleans the sewer water in Lincoln and most towns in Rhode Island.

By doing the readings we eliminated any wide swings between actual and estimated meter readings. It level loaded the bills and improved cash flow. This was great savings per month, we figure it saved us about $500-$700 per month.

My maintenance person made sure every apartment unit had no leaky faucets so water would not be wasted.

One interesting cost savings story related to the Schoolhouse involved a tenant named Tony. He was a gregarious character who thought he was much smarter than he was. He had a Section 8 voucher passed down through family generations. For the most part all of my Section 8 tenants feel fortunate and do not want to lose their voucher.

Tony was different in many ways.

The Section 8 tenant classification is based on the persons income and determines if the tenant has to pay for electric. Based on Tony's income we had to pay the electric for him.

We started fine, but it soon turned out to bet another tenant from hell.

He was habitually late making his monthly rent payment of $220 per month. Imagine $220 per month for rent and he cannot even pay the bill.

But while we were in the cost savings mode, we noticed something very unusual. Tony's electric bill was almost triple anyone else's in the building.

Well, the first time I entered the apartment I noticed an aquarium in the corner of the living room with a heat lamp attached to the metal rim of the aquarium. So I asked Tony what's in the aquarium and he politely mentioned that was his pet python snake. It was a 6-7 foot python.

He actually wore it around his neck to a meeting with the Section 8 coordinator.

Anyway, we served Tony papers for a court date due to late rent payment, but instead he moved out - but not before trashing the apartment.

To show you how bad he was, he put holes in the wall and burnt candle wax down the bathroom sink, tub and toilet. Not sure how, but my maintenance person knew how to get rid of it. Prior to that, I took pictures with my phone and sent it to every Section 8 housing coordinator in northern Rhode Island and told them never give Tony his voucher back that he lost during the court proceedings.

Today I heard Tony is living on the streets of Woonsocket. Like I said, he was not that smart.

Fortunately, we worked through the downtimes and came out of it with a much better real estate business. Rents started to increase again, and overall more folks needed housing.

The Gagnon's always taught me real estate was on a seven-year boon to bust cycle and this one ran pretty much true to form.

One of the main improvements we did at the Schoolhouse was to convert the whole building from oil to natural gas. One of the largest expenses was heating oil which we provided to the tenants. At one time it reached $4.50 per gallon during the downtimes. With interest rates still low we refinanced the schoolhouse for these improvements.

Our new bank accommodated us and I developed a relationship with a fine gentleman who was Vice President of Commercial Lending named Peter Murray. He was straight forward and did not play games as most of the bankers do.

Most bankers wanted your first born to get a loan with all the red tape, but during the housing collapse they were the problem giving loans out to folks who never really could afford them.

Anyway, we moved forward, but we soon quickly found out you really cannot do just one improvement. It turned out to be many. For example, to convert the building from oil to natural gas we had to apply for a permit to have National Grid run the gas line from the street to the meter on the house for a one time fee of $600.

There was an application process that could take forever, but luckily there was a gentleman named Louie Larose from Cranston. He was a fine gentleman who was a retired toolmaker from Woonsocket. We hung out together on Friday nights at Twin River betting the dog races and he looked at me like his son.

His son was up high at corporate in National Grid and my application got approved in two weeks. Once the construction crew ran the gas line up the side yard, only then would the heating contractor come in and run the line through the building.

With a building this size, we had two boiler rooms so they had to run the line the whole length of the building. As I previously stated, you cannot do just one improvement and this one was interesting.

There was a 1,000-gallon oil tank in the back parking lot. So to pull it out we had to have the soil tested and luckily it tested negative and there were no oil leaks. At this point in time, my commercial property insurer had written me up for the cracking driveway.

So we decided while we pulled out the oil tank, we might as well put in a new parking lot. I put out three bids and the best price with the same specifications was a guy named Lenny Johnson. He ran the business with his sons and had a great reputation.

Before we installed the new driveway my heating contractor recommended a company out of Pawtucket that pulls out oil tanks.

We hired them and one day in the pouring rain they pulled out this monstrous 1,000-gallon tank and we were ready to move onto the next phase.

Now, you know anything of this nature is never easy. On the side of the Schoolhouse was a strip of land owned by the Town of Lincoln which had an easement drain.

Over the years, the drain never worked properly and whenever there was a severe rainstorm in the winter it would drain onto the Schoolhouse parking lot and freeze to skating rink size. Tenant liability was an issue and the Department of Public Works (DPW) Director for the town saw the liability immediately.

He eventually hired my paving contractor Lenny and installed a pretty cool trough around the driveway to an easement drain in the corner of the property.

Once the driveway was installed, the heating contractor connected the gas lines to the building and we were heating with natural gas. We did this project in the fall and once the winter came we automatically derived approximately a 35% savings to our heating cost.

Another improvement you have to do when converting a building from oil to natural gas is to install new chimney flues due to wear and tear of the older bricks.

A chimney flue is basically a liner inside the chimney so that the heat can escape.

This made sense and increased the efficiency of the new natural gas burners.

Besides the insurance company writing us up for the uneven driveway they also mentioned the wrought iron railings around the building were out of date due to the new building codes. So we had three sections around the building replaced with new ones and we were done.

The investment cost around $75,000 so we figured about a five year payback, but we were here for the long haul anyway.

Remember in the previous chapter we talked about dead bodies? Well, this is one story worth telling.

The schoolhouse was a fairly easy property to manage since my wife had a real estate office where she would do the books and pay the bills.

Tenants would drop the rents through the mail slot in the door and my wife would record them and make deposits.

One night as I was sitting down for supper I received a call from one of the tenants stating there was a smell coming from the first-floor apartment and she thought someone was cooking an ethnic food that really had a nasty odor that just lingered throughout the common areas of the building.

So I decided to head down there and meet the tenant. Now with me showing up at 6 p.m. the rest of the tenants came out of their apartments to see what the commotion was.

First of all, the smell was nasty, so we determined it was coming from this one studio apartment. I knocked on the door, but got no answer. The tenant who lived there was a quiet gentleman who stayed to himself in the apartment and by day was a trader in the stock market.

As I opened the door, there was James naked by his computer desk.

Apparently, that smell was not ethnic food cooking, but a dead body that had been decomposing for four to five days.

Seeing the body was like something out of a horror movie, there were maggots all over it, even in its eyes.

Being a real estate person, I was never prepared to find or be in this situation. I surveyed the apartment closed the door and called the 911 emergency number. Within minutes state police, local police, rescue and the state medical examiner converged to the schoolhouse apartments.

By this time, my maintenance person came to the building my clothes smelled like death.

The body had been so decomposed that the bodily fluids had not only soiled the carpeting, but had gone into the sub-flooring.

Once this happens the medical examiner gives the owner of the building a list of cleaning companies that work for the state who specialize in these types of cleanups.

The expense ran into the thousands of dollars, so luckily I was covered by my commercial property insurance. The company did an excellent job and we rented this fully updated apartment for $50 more per month.

The gentleman that died was addicted to drugs and alcohol and was very sick and too young to die. That night when I got home my wife put all my clothes including shoes in a hefty trash bag and dumped it.

Want to hear another dead body story. Well here goes. This one was a little different and cleaner.

I rented a studio apartment to a young woman named Kathy, who was a military veteran of the Gulf War. She was very personable and had a good sense of humor.

It seemed like she had a good support system coming home and her family was always at the apartment visiting and taking her out to dinner.

As time went on she was an excellent tenant, a single woman who worked during the day, but other then her family kept to herself and turned out to be quite a loner.

One day I received a call from her sister stating she had tried to call Kathy, but no one answered the phone which was quite unusual.

So I decided to meet her at the apartment. When I opened the door, I found Kathy lying on the bathroom floor with a bottle of prescription drugs next to her.

One of the things we noticed was the body was not decomposed. It was frozen and maybe it was her training in the service, but Kathy opened all the windows fully in the apartment in the middle of February where the temperature averaged between 0 and 10 degrees.

Luckily there were no frozen pipes in this older brick building.

We called 911and within a matter of minutes the state police arrived to investigate in case it was a homicide.

As it turned out, Kathy committed suicide and was diagnosed with PTSD from her time in the military.

Chapter 7

Today

The schoolhouse property turned out to be a great investment based on increasing the gross rental income by 47%.

This GRI has increased the value from the original purchase price of $1 million to $1.8 million.

My family has grown with my daughter graduating from undergraduate and graduate programs and coming out of college with no loans.

She is currently a senior category manager for a jewelry / fashion accessory/ design firm, which is privately held in Rhode Island.

This year we helped her make her first investment in real estate and she bought a new end unit condo built in a 94 unit development in western Cranston.

We decided to sell the original investment, the 16-unit apartment building, to a fine younger gentleman who had 20 rental properties in southern Rhode Island.

The deal was not as easy as it sounded due to the fact mold had found it's way into the attic of the building.

We negotiated a settlement in which I would pay for the cleaning and he would give me a ten year monthly payment so I would not get taxed on any proceeds from the sale.

It worked out fine since the per unit price is what I wanted and the buyer avoided putting a large amount of down payment.

It was kind of sad letting that first investment go since it reminded me of the real estate agent named Lou Berthod who negotiated the deal for me with the funeral directors.

Between myself, the property manager and maintenance person we all learned the apartment rental business from that rundown property.

But, the property has fulfilled its useful life and worked for us to accomplish what we needed done.

My wife and I are now both retired from our professional jobs and we ended up selling the house in Greenville, Rhode Island, and bought one of the first condo units in an over-55 community.

It's a great place which has 2,100 square feet with a two car garage. Its professionally managed with a very reasonable HOA (homeowners association) fee.

It is centrally located in Lincoln RI and we say it's fifteen minutes from anywhere in Rhode Island.

We still manage 30 apartment rentals in two buildings and derive retirement income from both properties.

Remember the Gagnon's?

Roland recently called me from Florida where he is 82-years-old and wanted me to purchase his remaining units, which total 17 apartment rentals in three houses.

There are two six-unit buildings and one five-unit property.

I have already spoken to the bank and they will package these properties with my 12 units in Woonsocket which will include some seller financing to make the overall deal attractive for both of us.

This will give me 47 units to own and manage, which will be comfortable during our retirement years.

Chapter 8

Tips & Tricks of The Trade

Hopefully this book took some of the mystery out of real estate investing and offered some valuable real estate advice for the small investor.

Remember this business process will allow you to manage three or 300 residential units and be successful doing it.

Below I have put together a list of tricks and tips for those in the business or looking to get into it.

1. Find properties which are structurally sound but might need some cosmetic work. Structurally sound means the foundation is not cracked and/or sinking. Support beams are not decaying or there is any evidence of damage from termites. Electrical systems have been updated to latest building codes and the heating systems have a useful life.

2. Understand the fair market rent in the community. This is kind of a tricky one. One method I use to test the market is to advertise a vacancy at a very high price. This will show you if need to decrease the rent. If you rent it at the higher price, that's great.

3. For apartment turnovers apply three important elements : paint, flooring and appliances. As of today, these elements still apply. We usually paint the apartments with an off-white eggshell finish color with either dark or light carpeting and linoleum in the kitchen area.

One recommendation with paint is never do a room in pastel colors. It took us (10) gallons of paint later to remove the streaks.

4. Increase your rental marketability by including heat and hot water in the rent. Easier to rent and easier to increase rents.

Banks love the idea having tenants pay for everything since it makes the balance sheet good. The fact of the matter is managing a property with a mortgage your main priority is to keep all the apartments rented and avoid turnover costs.

5. Once equity is built refinance and pull the tax-free cash for either building improvements or use as a down payment for another rental property. Make your property work for you. Never use it for a Vegas trip or the purchased of an expensive automobile.

6. Allow pets in your property but no dogs larger than 50 pounds. Always do a Pet Addendum with the lease and charge a non-refundable fee. Never rent to tenants with exotic pets like the snake story.

7. Have an application process which asks the important questions and always run a credit, criminal or sex-offender background check. You can also go online to the state court system and enter any persons name to view court cases.

8. Develop good relationships with a heating contractor, electrician and a plumber. These folks are key to saving some money on the larger expenses.

9. Use lines of credit for the business whether it's secured or un-secured. Unsecured lines are great. They are not linked to any property and easier to pay down from the cash flow. I have had one for over 20 years.

10. Keep your properties looking neat with all trash picked up and landscaping neatly trimmed. This one is kind of self explanatory.

11. Develop a good relationship with a snowplow contractor and instruct them while it's snowing to make a first pass around the parking lot. After the snow stops have the contractor call you when he is coming back to finish the lot. You would then text all your tenants to move their vehicles so the lot will be cleared.

12. For any dead bodies call 911 emergency immediately. If body has decomposed use the State recommended cleaning companies.

13. Any potential tenant that wants to give you rental/security money very quickly hold off and run background checks. 99% of the time the tenant is a really bad one.

14. Work with community housing authorities and qualify good Section 8 tenants. Your rent is always deposited 1st of the month.

There is a fallacy that Section 8 tenants are usually bad but this one is not true. Majority of Section 8 tenants are very good since they do not want to lose that voucher.

15. Work with state agencies like the Department of Children and Families (DCYF) and Human Services. They always have folks that need to rent apartments and they will pay security and a couple of months rent.

16. When you advertise keep records of all the phone calls so when you have a vacancy you can fill it. I have always kept prior phone calls and whenever I had a vacancy those folks would be the first ones I call before putting an ad in the paper.

17. Keep detailed records by recording rent checks and provide rent receipts for anyone paying in cash or money orders.

Also anyone late on rent payment faithfully send out the five day demand letter post dated the 16th of the month. Do this the first month the rent is late. DO NOT WAIT.

This is the best method to evict and judge will usually give you possession of the apartment back.

18. Use excel spreadsheets to record income and expenses so every year you can give a thumbnail drive to your accountant. This makes it easy for you to explain recorded expenses during the year.

Also, remember for any large unforeseen capital expenses, record below the line as a one time charge.

www.ingramcontent.com/pod-product-compliance
Lightning Source LLC
Chambersburg PA
CBHW030050230526
45471CB00003B/1031